The Eiffel Tower

by Meg Greene

BLACKBIRCH®
PRESS

THOMSON
GALE

San Diego • Detroit • New York • San Francisco • Cleveland • New Haven, Conn. • Waterville, Maine • London • Munich

THOMSON

★

GALE

LIBRARY OF CONGRESS CATALOGING-IN-PUBLICATION DATA

Greene, Meg.
  The Eiffel Tower / by Meg Greene.
    p. cm. — (Building world landmarks)
  Summary: Describes the techniques used and difficulties faced in building the Eiffel Tower, once the tallest building in the world and still an extremely popular tourist attraction.
  Includes bibliographical references and index.
    ISBN 1-56711-315-X
  1. Tour Eiffel (Paris, France)—Juvenile literature. 2. Civil engineering—France—Paris—History—Juvenile literature. [1. Eiffel Tower (Paris, France) 2. Civil engineering.] I. Title. II. Series.

    TA149.G74 2004
    725'.97'0944361—dc21

                                                    2003001494

Printed in the United States
10 9 8 7 6 5 4 3 2 1

Table of Contents

Introduction
Towers: Reaching for the Heavens 5

Chapter 1
The Search for a Tower 9

Chapter 2
The Design 19

Chapter 3
Construction Begins 25

Chapter 4
Racing Against the Clock 33

Chapter 5
The Dedication 39

Chronology 45

Glossary 46

For More Information 47

Index 48

Towers: Reaching for the Heavens

EVEN THOUGH THEY are common today, the sight of tall buildings can still be exhilarating. In almost every major city around the world, there are at least one or two buildings that tower over others and are landmarks by which the city is known: the Empire State Building in New York City, the Sears Tower in Chicago, the Transamerica Pyramid Building in San Francisco, the Space Needle in Seattle, the CN Tower in Toronto, the Petronas Towers in Kuala Lumpur, and the Ostakino Tower in Moscow, to name just a few. These monuments of steel, glass, and concrete are marvels of modern construction. Although many persons think of tall buildings as products of the twentieth century, the idea of building skyscrapers is not new at all. Since ancient times, people have dreamed of constructing structures that rose majestically toward the heavens. These tall buildings are also known as towers and are

Opposite:
Visitors to Paris are always awed by their first glimpse of the Eiffel Tower.

5

characterized not only by their great height, but by the fact that their height is much greater than their width.

Throughout history, many different cultures have built towers of one sort or another. For example, among the very first towers were the ziggurats, or "heavenly mountains," built in ancient Mesopotamia as early as 3000 B.C. These structures, which were used as religious temples, usually measured 200 feet by 150 feet at the base and rose to upwards of 70 feet. Another famous tower was the Tower of Babel, thought to have been built somewhere in Babylon. It is estimated to have been one of the tallest structures of its time, standing approximately 300 feet high.

By the Middle Ages, builders were constructing even taller towers with the help of skeletal framing that provided a sturdy framework with which to build. A common type of tower built during this period was the campanile, or large bell tower, attached to many churches and monasteries. Towers were also attached to castles and forts as lookout posts that offered protection from one's enemies.

By the late nineteenth century, as building technology improved, new materials such as iron, steel, and reinforced concrete made it possible to design and construct even grander structures. Building tall buildings soon became something of an international competition, with architects from around the world vying to build the tallest structure. These buildings came to symbolize a new age of technological and industrial progress. It was against this historical background that the spectacular Eiffel Tower was built.

From the first, the tower proved an awesome sight. It became and remains the most recognizable image of Paris and, indeed, of France. Although critics at the time of its construction and since dismissed it as a monstrosity, the Eiffel Tower has captured the hearts of residents and tourists alike, many of whom come from the world over to see it. Its image has been reproduced on everything from postage stamps to candles to amusement park attractions.

Although now dwarfed by many larger buildings, the Eiffel Tower remains the tallest tower ever constructed. The Eiffel Tower also stands as a symbol of modernity, an exciting blend of technology and art. In 1964, the French government at last declared officially what the French and many people around the world already knew: The Eiffel Tower was a historical monument without peer. The tower today is a recognized architectural landmark and is also considered to be one of the Seven Modern Wonders of the World.

Chapter 1

The Search for a Tower

IN FRANCE, THE last two decades of the late nineteenth century are known as the "Belle Epoque," or the "beautiful years." For many French men and women, this period of great prosperity was a welcome relief from the horrors of only ten years before. In 1870–1871, France had been defeated in the Franco-Prussian War, which was followed by a horrifying civil uprising that left much of Paris in ruins and thousands dead.

Things could not have been more different by 1878. Peace had returned; people had jobs and, as a result, more money to spend. Nowhere was this affluence more evident than in Paris. The city bustled with energy. Cafes were filled with men and women meeting to talk, drink, and dine. The theaters and opera house did a brisk business. Even the parks were filled with people strolling, picnicking, boating, or just taking in the sights.

Opposite:
The French government invited designs for a structure that would showcase French technology and engineering.

9

August Renoir's painting, Le Moulin de la Galette, *depicted the Belle Epoque of the late 1800s, during which Parisians enjoyed a period of peace and prosperity.*

During the Belle Epoque, France was also on the verge of reclaiming its place among the great powers of Europe. Although most French citizens were content, the French government was dissatisfied. It wanted to find ways to celebrate French history, culture, progress, and power. French leaders wanted to send a message to the rest of Europe that France was once again important.

The Idea of an Exposition

As early as 1878, officials of the French government began to discuss the best ways to commemorate the centennial of the French Revolution, which would occur in 1889. Although some officials thought the centennial celebration should not be too grand or fancy, others disagreed. They wanted to hold an extravagant industrial exposition, or fair, to commemorate not only the past, but also to celebrate the glorious future that they believed was in store for France. An industrial exposition would showcase the great advances the French had made in technology and engineering.

One of the most enthusiastic supporters of such an exposition was French prime minister Jules Ferry. Ferry believed that such an event would demonstrate that French engineering and technology was among the best in the world. He believed so much in this idea that he convinced French president Jules Grévy to support it. On November 8, 1884, Grévy signed a decree proclaiming that a "Universal Exposition of the Products of Industry" would open in Paris on May 5, 1889, and would continue until October 31. The French government hoped that its exposition would be one of the most successful and memorable ever staged.

Planning the Exhibition

Even though the exposition was meant to celebrate the centennial of the French Revolution, the emphasis of the exposition was to be on French technology. French officials reasoned that by highlighting French technological and economic progress rather than the French Revolution, the exposition might draw more participants. They realized that other European nations viewed their country with distrust. This attitude was,

This painting by Paul Delaroche depicts events in the French Revolution. It was a time of violence and radical political activity in France.

in part, due to the violence that took place during and after the French Revolution—violence that did not remain confined to France but spread to the rest of Europe. France was also a hotbed of radical political activity. Still, the Exposition Committee hoped to make their event so appealing that people from other countries would be eager to participate to show off their latest technological and engineering accomplishments.

Unfortunately, the first responses were disappointing: The governments of Austria-Hungary, Belgium, Great Britain, the Netherlands, and Germany, not wishing to take part in an event that celebrated the

French Revolution, all refused the invitation. A number of private citizens from these countries, however, organized their own exhibits and, without sponsorship from their governments, sent them to what became known as the French Centennial Exposition.

By 1886, with a working budget of $8.6 million, French officials were ready to begin construction, but some felt the exposition lacked a central attraction. They sought some sort of monumental exhibit to show the world the great achievements of French technology and engineering.

The Idea of a Tower

Édouard Lockroy, the minister of commerce and industry and the chairman of the Exposition Committee, was the first to propose the construction of a 1,000-foot tower as a fitting emblem for the fair. He wanted to build a structure that was almost twice the height of what was then the tallest tower in the world, the Washington Monument. Begun during the 1840s but completed in 1884, the obelisk-shaped monument soared to the then-astonishing height of 555 feet. The Exposition Committee embraced Lockroy's idea with enthusiasm and decided to hold a competition to select a design.

On May 2, 1886, the *Journal Officiel,* the official publication of the French government, invited all French architects and engineers to submit designs for the buildings and other attractions at the exposition. In addition, the government invited entrants to submit designs for Lockroy's tower. The committee gave the contestants specific guidelines: The tower was to be approximately 1,000 feet tall with a base no more than 410 feet square and was to be built on the Champ de Mars, a popular park in central Paris. Although the committee promised to consider designs that did not meet these specifications, the advertisement made it clear that the committee, and especially Lockroy, wished for a big tower, specifically a metal one, to display French technological and engineering prowess.

As if the technical challenge were not enough to attract the best architects and engineers, the committee announced that it would award cash prizes for the twelve best designs. Applicants did not have much time—the deadline for submissions was May 18, only a scant two weeks after the advertisement appeared in the *Journal Officiel*. Despite the tight deadline, more than one hundred proposals arrived for review.

The Winner!

During the next few weeks, the committee reviewed each design. One design in particular appeared to fill all the requirements that Lockroy wanted. By June 12, less than a month after the competition began, the committee made a decision. The winner of the eight-hundred-dollar first prize was Gustave Eiffel, a fifty-three-year-old architectural engineer. Already considered one of the finest and most innovative architectural engineers in France, Eiffel had planned his boldest project yet. His winning design consisted of an iron tower that would stand nearly one thousand feet high and weigh approximately seven thousand tons. Construction would also be expensive, with estimated

costs totaling $1.6 million or approximately $34 million in current dollars.

Before making their selection, the committee had to decide whether Eiffel's design could, in fact, be constructed at the Champ de Mars. In proposing his design,

Before the Eiffel Tower was built, the Washington Monument was the tallest tower in the world.

Gustave Eiffel won eight hundred dollars for his design of a one thousand-foot metal tower to be built on the Champ de Mars.

Eiffel had argued that using stone or masonry would be too expensive and take too long. He impressed the committee with his revolutionary plan to use metal to build the tower. The committee could not resist the possibilities that this tower presented. If Eiffel succeeded, the tower would be the crown jewel of the exposition and a fitting symbol of French engineering genius.

Designing and Building a Tower

To prepare for the construction of the tower, Eiffel had his draftsmen draw blueprints for every single piece of metal that was to be used. In all, 5,329 mechanical drawings were done, representing 18,038 separate items of the tower. These drawings were done by a group of thirty draftsmen and took eighteen months to complete. The drawings covered 14,352 square feet of paper, roughly the size a soccer playing field.

Eiffel knew he was in a race against time. In order to adhere to the tight deadline, he created a strict construction schedule. To make construction more efficient, Eiffel had each piece of the tower created in a workshop located approximately three miles from the building site. At Eiffel's shop, workers produced more than four hundred tons of girders, beams, and trusses, which were special frames used to strengthen structures. From there, horse-drawn wagons carried the materials to the construction site, where workmen lifted them into place with the help of a steam-powered

Eiffel conducted many experiments to find the exact pressure the tower would exert against its foundation.

crane. In addition, every one of the 2.5 million holes in which special pins called rivets would be placed were also drawn in to ensure accuracy. Twenty teams of riveters drilled the majority of holes before individual pieces ever left the shop. Workers then drilled the remaining holes after they had hoisted each piece into place.

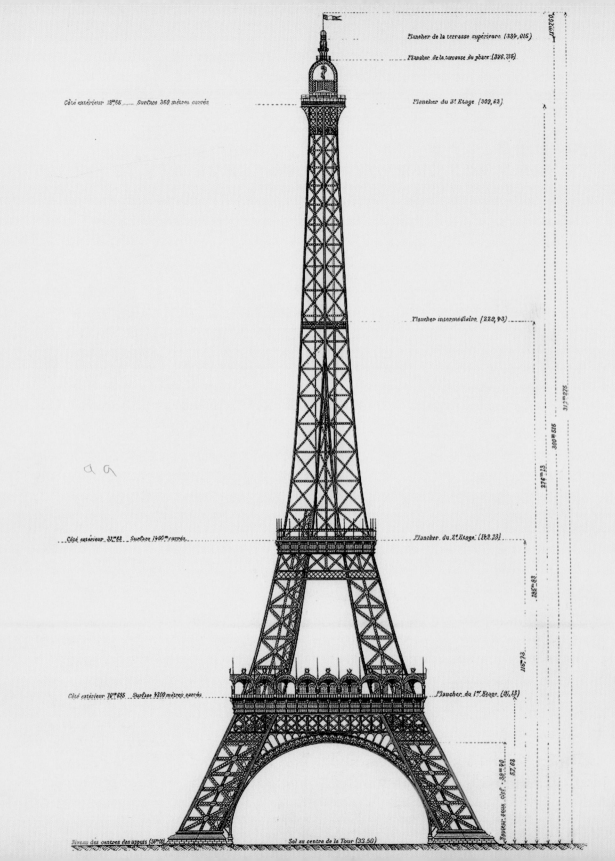

Plancher de la terrasse supérieure (334,015)

Plancher de la terrasse du phare (326,715)

Côté extérieur 18ᵐ65 _____ Surface 350 mètres carrés

Plancher du 3ᵉ Étage (303,63)

Plancher intermédiaire (228,43)

Côté extérieur 31ᵐ83 _____ Surface 1400ᵐ carrés.

Planchers du 2ᵉ Étage. (143,23)

Côté extérieur 70ᵐ685 _____ Surface 4200 mètres carrés

Plancher du 1ᵉʳ Étage. (81,13)

Niveau des centres des appuis (36ᵐ00)

Sol au centre de la Tour (33.50)

The Design

ON JANUARY 8, 1887, Gustave Eiffel signed a sixteen-page document that stated the terms of his commission to build a tower for the exposition. The contract, which Éduoard Lockroy, representing the national government, and Eugène Poubelle, representing the city of Paris, also signed, outlined the methods for financing the construction and the conditions for running the tower when construction was completed. Under the terms of the agreement, the French government would pay 1.5 million francs, or roughly $4 million in current dollars, to fund the construction. While that was a large sum of money, it fell short of the projected 6.5 million francs Eiffel estimated he needed to complete construction. To raise the rest of the money, Eiffel formed his own company, becoming, in effect, part owner of the tower that was to bear his name.

Under the terms of the contract, Eiffel was to have his tower completed by the time the exposition opened

Opposite:
This reproduction of the original design blueprint shows the elevations of various points of the tower.

19

in 1889. He was to build the tower on the site chosen by the committee located in the Champ de Mars. To help offset Eiffel's costs, the city of Paris and the Exposition Committee agreed to let Eiffel receive any income that came from the tower during the exhibition. In addition, when the exhibition closed, the city of Paris was to take ownership of the tower, though Eiffel would still receive income from it. With the contract signed and Eiffel formally taking possession of the construction site, work on the tower could begin.

A Unique Design

The design Eiffel submitted to the Exposition Committee was a masterpiece of late-nineteenth-century technology. The base of the tower was to consist of four wrought-iron legs resting atop four large stone piers, or large square or rectangular posts, that would support the entire weight of the tower. The tower would have three levels, including a 45,200-square-foot gallery on the first level, a 9,700-square-foot gallery on the second level, and, on the third level, a 2,700-square-foot dome surrounded by an external balcony. This last area would provide not only a spectacular view of Paris, but, as Eiffel saw it, could be used to conduct scientific experiments as well. To make the tower even more inviting, Eiffel also proposed opening restaurants on the first level where people could take in the Paris skyline while dining.

Eiffel's design was not only unique, it was also groundbreaking. In keeping with the spirit of the exposition, Eiffel wanted his tower to demonstrate how

the new types of building materials that were now available could be used. He also wished to showcase new engineering techniques.

Although the idea of a tall tower was not new, the manner in which Eiffel proposed to build it was. For instance, instead of using stone, the material that was commonly used to build tall structures, Eiffel thought the tower ought to be built of more modern materials

Eiffel designed four wrought-iron legs to support the seventy-three-hundred-ton tower.

21

such as wrought iron, cast iron, or steel. All three of these materials had been developed during the mid– to late nineteenth century and were prized for their strength and durability.

Eiffel finally decided on wrought iron. Of all the available materials, it was the heaviest and the least likely to buckle; cast iron was strong but more brittle and could break apart. Wrought iron stood up well against the elements and was more pliable than cast iron, which made it easier to work with. At the same time, wrought iron was less costly than steel. Like cast iron, steel was not sturdy enough for Eiffel's tower.

Challenging the Wind

One of the biggest problems that Eiffel faced was how to protect the tower from high winds, so he designed the tower to be wind resistant. He decided to build a series of lattice-trussed piers, or legs, that curved inward and would rest on top of the stone piers. These legs would effectively cut down wind resistance because they would be more aerodynamic. The tower would be able to withstand heavy winds without the danger of collapsing.

In addition to strengthening the tower against potentially dangerous winds, Eiffel's lattice-trussed supports provided increased stability. This was particularly important since the estimated weight of the tower was approximately seven thousand tons. Eiffel was also concerned that the stone piers could not support the weight of the tower alone. If the piers collapsed, the structure would crumple and fall.

A Great Challenge

Eiffel had taken great care in preparing his design. He was precise in his calculations, making sure that every piece of metal fit together and that every bolt fit neatly into its hole. On paper, it appeared that everything was in place and would work. The challenge would be for Eiffel to turn his design and his theories into reality.

Not everyone appreciated Eiffel's efforts or his tower. Critics of the tower design argued that it was impractical and that Eiffel's ideas could not work in real life. What Eiffel proposed had never been done; others had tried to build tall towers and failed. Further, critics pointed out, for Eiffel's tower to stand, his measurements could not be off, even by four one-thousandths of an inch. To achieve this level of precision seemed impossible.

There was also the matter of the timetable for construction. The exposition was scheduled to open in the spring of 1889, which meant that Eiffel had only two years to complete the tower. Skeptics pointed out that the Washington Monument, which was not nearly as massive as the Eiffel Tower, took more than thirty-six years to complete. Many doubted that Eiffel could build a structure more than twice the size in just two years.

Even as the debate over the tower continued, Eiffel went over his plans again to make sure he had accounted for everything. Although he defended his vision and his design, he knew that his words would not quiet critics. To silence those who doubted his ideas and abilities, Eiffel had to do more than talk about his tower. He had to build it.

Chapter 3

Construction Begins

BY JANUARY 1887, Gustave Eiffel was prepared to break ground for the construction of his tower. Just as construction got underway, however, he discovered a new problem. Earlier, he had ordered soil samples to be taken of the area in which the tower was to be built. The samples indicated that the land to the south and east consisted of clay covered by a thick layer of gravel, which was an ideal base to support such a heavy structure. To his dismay, however, he learned that the soil to the north and west was completely different. Here, it was mostly wet sand, clay, and mud, which made for a soggy, mucky soil that would provide a poor foundation.

Problems with the soil delayed the start of construction. After he studied the soil and looked over the site, Eiffel decided to use two different construction techniques to anchor the piers. For the south and

Opposite:
Hydraulic jacks were installed in the base of each column to hoist the six thousand- pound iron girders. This picture shows the progress of construction in September 1888.

25

Workers on the west side of the tower had to work carefully because they were digging below the water level of the Seine River.

east foundations, Eiffel had workers set the foundations into the gravel and hard clay. For the area near the river, Eiffel determined that if they dug the river-side foundations sixteen feet deeper than the dry-side foundations to the east and south, then the piers would eventually come to rest on a more solid clay foundation. The workers could set the foundations without the fear that they would sink or give way.

When the excavations were complete, Eiffel ordered workers to prepare the foundations. He had designed each pier to rest on a massive pile of cement and stone, which Eiffel directed to be set at an angle.

The piles were angled because the curving columns that would bear the weight of the tower would exert their force at right angles and would then be more stable. If the piles were simply built straight up and down, the columns would not be able to sustain the heavy weight of the tower and would collapse. By the end of June, Eiffel and his construction crews had laid the foundation for the tower. In five months, Eiffel's men had positioned and set the 180-foot cement and limestone piers. The workers dug carefully, especially

The Eiffel Tower rests on four 180-foot cement-and-limestone piers.

on the west side of the tower, where the bases would have to be set below the water level of the Seine River and where there would likely be problems with water seepage. Even though construction had only begun, Parisians could see the tower progressing.

A New Building Technology

Eiffel broke new ground in architectural engineering in the way he placed the iron braces, which were a type of metal supports. The iron girders weighed approximately three tons each, and Eiffel needed somehow to maneuver them into place. By installing hydraulic jacks in the iron base of each column, workers could place the iron trusses with precision.

As the tower crept slowly toward the sky, Eiffel installed four simultaneous hoisting systems, including steam winches, which are steam-powered machines used for pulling or lifting heavy weights, and swiveling creeper cranes. The creeper cranes were machines that could lift and lower a load, as well as move loads horizontally. Mounted on sloping tracks much like railroad tracks located inside the piers, the cranes traveled up and down from the ground to the tower frame. They not only carried construction materials from the ground to platforms where workers waited, but they were also mobile. They could pivot a full 360 degrees and could be moved up the tower as the building progressed. Without the creeper cranes, Eiffel could never have built the tower, for it would otherwise have been impossible to move materials from the ground to such great heights.

The Tower Takes Shape

By early October, the tower stood at 92 feet. Before construction crews could go any higher, though, they had to place temporary scaffolding around the completed sections of the tower. The scaffolding would provide additional support and prevent the tower from leaning, or worse, from falling over. Once the scaffolding was in place, workers built four platforms that were 150 feet high and 82 feet long, located in the inside center of each side of the tower. When joined, they formed a wood square. This frame would not only help to offset the increasing weight that came to bear as the tower continued to rise, but would also serve as a platform to

Construction began in January 1887. By the time this picture was taken on March 26, 1888, Eiffel was convinced that the tower would neither lean nor fall over.

support the heavy iron girders and trusses needed to complete the next section of the tower.

In addition to the scaffolding, Eiffel also had twelve wooden, derrick-shaped pylons built. These ninety-foot-tall pylons were to be used as hoisting machines, with each pylon located beneath the twelve interior columns spaced among the tower's four piers. A set of hydraulic jacks, which were special machines used to move heavy objects short distances, were also attached to the base of each column.

Using this design and machinery, Eiffel then devised a system to correct the angle of each pier. A sand-filled metal cylinder rested on top of each pylon and attached to each column. Each cylinder had a piston at the top and a plug at the bottom. With these pylons, Eiffel could adjust the angle of each pier. If a column was found to be too high, the plug at the bottom of the cylinder was pulled, which allowed sand to run out until the piston and the column were lowered to the correct position. If a column was too low, the jack beside the cylinder could be operated to push the column to the proper angle.

Eiffel also arranged for an additional crane to be installed on the first-level platform and situated small wagons that looked like miniature boxcars on tracks placed around the perimeter of the platform. The crane now lifted building materials from the ground level and placed them into the wagons. The wagons rolled the materials to one of the four creeper cranes, which, in turn, lifted the materials to workers waiting on the next level. By using these methods and working his crews longer and harder than ever, Eiffel completed the second level of the tower by July 1888. The tower now stood 380 feet high. But Eiffel still had a long way to go before the tower was complete, and time was running out.

New Building Technology

Eiffel's decision to use wrought iron in building his tower was yet another use found for this old and versatile metal. Wrought iron began to take the place of bronze in Asia Minor as far back as the second millennium B.C. The metal was used for a variety of purposes, from making tools for farming to weaponry. Early on, it was discovered that one of the chief advantages of iron was that it was far more available than copper or tin, metals that were also used to make tools and weapons. As a building material, wrought iron gained wider use beginning in the nineteenth century. It was created by reheating and reshaping iron bars. Wrought iron was especially useful in the construction of bridges: The elastic qualities that allowed it to stretch and bend made wrought iron especially effective when it came to wind resistance, because wrought iron can give and bend just enough to handle large gusts of wind. But with the invention of the Bessemer and open-hearth processes in the mid–nineteenth century, wrought iron was overtaken by steel as the most desirable material in building construction. Yet, wrought iron has not disappeared entirely. Today it is often used for decorative purposes such as on railings, doors, balconies, and grilles.

Chapter 4

Racing Against the Clock

DESPITE THE PROGRESS he had made, Eiffel knew he could not let up. He had less than a year to complete the tower, and every minute counted. His workmen, who at the beginning of the project had toiled for nine or ten hours a day, now worked up to twelve hours a day, seven days a week.

In order to finish the tower on time, Eiffel realized that he needed once again to create a new method of building. He had struggled with what would be the best way to build from the second level to the top of the tower. The four piers that separated the first and second levels needed to be drawn together to create a single vertical column that tapered toward the top of the tower.

The creeper cranes on which Eiffel had relied so heavily to finish the first two stages were of no use to him now. Given their size and weight, he could find

Opposite:
The second level was completed by July 1888, but with less than a year to go, crews began working twelve hours a day, seven days a week in order to finish on time.

no way to attach them to the tower beyond the second level. To solve his dilemma, Eiffel placed smaller, fifty-ton creeper cranes on the vertical beams that rose from the center of the tower. He positioned the cranes back-to-back so that they counterbalanced each other. This arrangement also made it possible for the workers to reach the cranes. Eiffel provided additional support to the cranes by adding thirty-foot-by-twelve-foot iron frames, bolted to the central beams, to which he had the cranes attached.

To complete the top of the tower, crews worked on one thirty-foot section at a time. After completing work on one section, they moved on to the next, each time reattaching the cranes and building upward. Each section took only about thirty hours to complete. To keep up the steady pace, Eiffel installed four hoisting systems that lifted materials almost continuously. Using a steam winch to lift materials from the ground to the first level, Eiffel employed a second steam winch to transport materials to the second platform. From there, a third winch carried material to a platform situated 650 feet above the ground. The last winch brought the materials to the creeper cranes. Eiffel's system proved effective: The entire process of raising materials from ground level to the highest elevation took only about twenty minutes, an amazing feat by nineteenth-century standards.

The Elevators

One of the greatest challenges in the construction of the tower was its elevator system, which had to ac-

This elevator, installed on the first level during construction, is still used by visitors today.

commodate four hundred persons at three different platforms. Eiffel wanted a system that would be fast and efficient as well as pleasing to the eye. Construction of the elevators was also the only job that Eiffel had to subcontract. Because he had relatively little control over this aspect of construction, it left him more nervous and frustrated than any other.

In part, Eiffel's concerns arose because the elevator industry was in its infancy, and he had misgivings about installing the new hydraulic lifts, which had been in use for only a decade. Yet Eiffel also knew that elevators were absolutely necessary. Visitors might be willing to climb the 363 steps from the ground level to the first platform, but few would be willing to ascend the additional 381 steps to the second level. The top of the tower, although not open to the public, would only be accessible by elevator. After all, staff personnel could not be expected to climb the 927 steps from the second level. For people to enjoy visiting and working in the tower, therefore, a safe and efficient elevator system was indispensable.

Like so many other aspects of the tower construction, however, installing elevators would not be easy. Complicating the situation were the tower's angled legs. The elevator cars could not be housed in a simple vertical shaft, but would have to travel on specially curved tracks. For his purposes, Eiffel needed the best and most reliable equipment money could buy. He hired three elevator companies, each of which provided a portion of the needed machinery for the tower. The French company of Roux, Combaluzier, and Lepape installed elevators to run from the ground to the first level in the east and west pillars. In the north pillar, an American company, Otis Elevators, installed an elevator that went directly from ground level to the second level. A second Otis elevator, located in the south pillar, operated between the first and second levels. Finally, another French firm, the Edoux Company, built the elevator that ran between the second and third platforms. This arrangement worked well and accomplished the primary goal: the installation of reliable elevators. The tower was now almost complete.

Eiffel's Solution

On January 26, 1887, workmen began the difficult task of digging the tower's foundations. To make as efficient use of his men and time as possible, Eiffel came up with an ingenious scheme. He had his metal shops construct a number of watertight containers made of sheet metal. These containers, also known as caissons, would allow the workers to remove the dirt. Each caisson measured fifty feet in length, twenty feet in width, and ten feet in depth, with four caissons used for each foundation leg. Each caisson had a work chamber approximately six feet high that allowed several men to work with shovels and pickaxes. Entering the caisson through a top air lock, the men would collect the dirt in buckets that they then passed through the air lock. To help bore through the earth, the caissons were designed with wedge-shaped walls.

Workers in caissons removed dirt to build the foundation.

The Dedication

Only in early 1889 did Eiffel begin to feel confident that he would meet the committee's deadline, but there were still a few things left to do to prepare for opening day. For instance, on the first level, where Eiffel expected the majority of visitors, he added a rectangular promenade, or walkway, 930 feet long and 9 feet wide with nine decorative arches on either side. Here the public would receive its first grand view of the tower. Now that the construction was nearly finished, Eiffel had the tower painted. Using the color Barbados bronze, a reddish brown, Eiffel instructed the painters to apply the paint in gradually lighter shades from the bottom to the top, a technique he hoped would make the tower seem even taller than it was.

Then, incredibly, it was over. By the end of March 1889, nearly six weeks before the exposition was to open, the Eiffel Tower stood complete. Its final height

Opposite:
During the six-month Centennial Exposition in 1889, almost 2 million people visited the Eiffel Tower.

was recorded at 986 feet, the tallest structure in the world at that time. If laid on its side, the tower would extend almost a quarter of a mile. The base of the tower covered two and a half acres, while the overall weight of tower was approximately seventy-three hundred tons—about the same weight as 1,042 male elephants or of approximately 79 B-S2 airplanes. To ascend to the tower by foot, a person would climb 1,671 steps.

Eiffel had not only made his deadline but kept construction costs under budget. Finally, to add to the growing list of his amazing accomplishments, Eiffel had built the tower with almost no loss of life. Only one fatality had occurred during the construction, when a young worker, eager to impress his girlfriend, had fallen to his death from the first-floor platform just as the bell sounded to end the workday.

More than Just a Tower

Visitors to the Eiffel Tower could do more than just take in the view. They could shop, often purchasing souvenirs of the tower and the exposition. They could dine at one of the four restaurants located in the tower, each of which offered a different type of cuisine.

The offices located in the tower, which Eiffel offered for rent, already had new tenants. The French newspaper *Le Figaro,* which planned to publish a special daily during the exposition, had leased offices on the second floor. A pub and pastry shop also readied to open.

Those visitors willing to brave the dizzying heights of almost one thousand feet could ascend to the octagonal-shaped third level. This area, which was completely enclosed in glass, offered a stunning view of the exposition and the city of Paris while protecting visitors from the elements. From this level, visitors often took notice of a short spiral staircase that was off-limits to the general public. Beyond the stairs was a small apartment in which Gustave Eiffel now made his home.

Spotlights were placed near the top of the tower to illuminate monuments around Paris.

Two powerful spotlights attached to a small balcony surrounding the third platform of the tower entertained those who visited the exposition at night. Mounted on a small track, the lights could be moved to illuminate the different monuments located throughout Paris. Positioned at the very top of the tower was an electric beacon, or light, with a range of nearly 120 miles. Enclosed by a cylinder that contained prisms of red, white, and blue, the colors of the French flag, an electric lamp was timed to flash every ninety seconds. To protect the tower from lightning, Eiffel had eight lightning rods installed.

Opening Day

On Sunday, March 31, 1889, a dedication ceremony was held at the newly completed Eiffel Tower. After the brief celebration, a large French flag was raised to the top of the tower. Shortly after the ceremony, a violent spring storm arose, pelting the city with heavy rains and strong winds. Many waited anxiously to see how the new tower would stand up against the weather. When they looked upward, they saw the flag waving furiously, but the tower stood.

To almost no one's surprise, the tower emerged as the most popular attraction at the exposition. Huge crowds waited in line for hours to be allowed to climb it, ride to the top, and dine in one of its cafés. By the close of the exposition almost six months later, nearly 2 million people had visited the Eiffel Tower. On average almost eleven thousand people a day came, with the single largest turnout on June 10, 1889, when a record twenty-three thousand people visited.

Taking Care of the Tower

Keeping the tower in good shape is expensive. On average, five hundred thousand dollars is spent annually on maintenance and upkeep. This amount includes the salaries of 119 persons, including 2 full-time engineer supervisors and 37 technicians. The remaining 80 workers operate the elevators, sell and take tickets, and make sure that everything operates smoothly on each platform. Occasionally, sections of the tower need to be repaired or replaced. When that happens, workers use special closed-circuit televisions to pinpoint the areas that need work. Going carefully over every bolt and rivet helps the engineers to make precise evaluations of the strength and stability of the tower. Every seven years, the tower receives a new coat of paint. To paint the tower, or "give her a new dress" as the Parisians say, is the single largest maintenance job done to the tower. Thirty professional painters are hired for the

The Eiffel Tower gets a new coat of paint every seven years.

job. First they scrub off the grime and then sand and touch up any rust spots. Next comes the application of fifty-five tons of a special silicon and lead paint to protect the tower until its next paint job.

Thousands of "towerists" visit the Eiffel Tower each month, making it one of the world's most popular tourist attractions.

A Most Famous Landmark

Gustave Eiffel often joked that his tower was more famous than he was. Since it opened more than one hundred years ago, the Eiffel Tower has attracted a steady stream of visitors and continues to be the largest attraction in Paris and throughout France. In fact, the people who come to visit the Eiffel Tower have even received a special nickname from the French press. They are now known not as tourists, but as "towerists."

The Eiffel Tower is one of the most imaginative and fascinating structures in the world. It stands in silent tribute to its gifted designer whose vision and skill allowed people to come a little closer to reaching the heavens.

Chronology

1832   Gustave Alexandre Eiffel born in Dijon, France, on December 15.

1866   Eiffel founds construction company, Eiffel Inc. From 1866 to 1869, Eiffel designs bridges in France, Spain, Austria, Egypt, and Peru.

1886   Gustave Eiffel wins design competition for the 1889 French Centennial Exposition.

1887   Construction begins.

1889   The tower is completed almost two months ahead of schedule.

1921   First European public radio broadcast is done from the tower.

1923   Gustave Eiffel dies at the age of ninety-one.

1940   The tower is closed to all but German soldiers during the German occupation.

1953   France's first television station begins operations from the Eiffel Tower.

1989   The tower's one-hundredth anniversary is celebrated; more than 5 million people visit.

1999   The Eiffel Tower hosts a spectacular millennium celebration.

Glossary

caisson—A watertight chamber in which underwater construction can be done.

cast iron—A hard, brittle iron made with carbon used for structural and decorative construction.

gallery—A long, narrow hallway; a building or hall used for displays.

hydraulic—Through the use of pressure, the moving of liquids such as water or oil through pipes.

hydraulic presses—Machinery using hydraulic power for construction.

lattice girders—Metal beams that consist of diagonal pieces crisscrossing each other in a lattice work pattern.

lattice trusses—Two parallel metal beams linked by small metal bars arranged in a zigzag pattern.

masonry—Constructed of stone or brick.

piers—Square or rectangular posts or supports often made of masonry or wood that carry the weight of the entire structure.

prefabricated—Built or manufactured parts made in advance.

rivet—A metal bolt or nail.

truss—A type of bracing or framework, often found in bridges.

Books

Winnie Denker and Françoise Sagan, *The Eiffel Tower*. New York: Vendome Press, 1989.

Henri Loyrette, *Gustave Eiffel*. New York: Rizzoli, 1985.

Periodicals

Jean-Pierre Navailles, "Eiffel's Tower," *History Today*, December 1989.

Websites

Eiffel Tower (www.greatbuildings.com). From the Great Buildings site, this Web page contains photos and brief facts about the tower.

Eiffel Tower Web Page (www.endex.com). This Web page is full of news, facts, and information about the tower.

Official Site of the Eiffel Tower (www.tour-eiffel.fr). Find out how many people have visited the tower since it first opened, its history, and other interesting bits of information. The site also provides information on the tower's hours of operation and ticket prices.

Tour Eiffel (www.paris.org). This Web page contains a brief overview of and facts about the tower.

Index

Belle Epoque, 9, 10
building materials, 6–7, 21–22
building technology, 7, 28–31, 33–34

caissons, 36
campanile, 6
Centennial Exposition, 13, 42
Champ de Mars, 14, 15, 20
creeper cranes, 28, 30, 33–34

dedication, 39–44

Eiffel, Gustave, 14, 17, 19, 41, 44
Eiffel Tower
    construction, 17, 25–31
    design of, 17, 19–23
    financing for, 19
    inside the, 40–41

maintenance for, 43
opening day of, 42
ownership of, 20
statistics of, 20, 40
technology of, 33–34
timetable for, 23, 33
elevators, 34–36
exposition, 10–13

foundation, 25–27, 36
French Centennial Exposition, 13, 42
French Revolution, 11–12

hoisting system, 28, 30, 34

Lockroy, Édouard, 13, 14, 19

metal, 14, 16, 17, 31

paint, 39, 43
Paris, 7, 9, 20, 44
promenade, 39

restaurants, 20, 40
rivets, 17

scaffolding, 29–30
Seven Modern Wonders of the World, 7
skyscrapers, 5
spotlights, 41–42
steps, 36, 40

technology, 7, 11–13, 20, 28–31
Tower of Babel, 6
towerists, 44
towers, 5–6, 7, 13

visitors, 39, 42, 44

Washington Monument, 13, 23
wind, 22, 31, 42
wrought iron, 22, 31

ziggurats, 6